£2 95

Watching The Moon Landing

by

Phil Vernon

First published 2022 by The Hedgehog Poetry Press

Published in the UK by
The Hedgehog Poetry Press
5, Coppack House
Churchill Avenue
Clevedon
BS21 6QW

www.hedgehogpress.co.uk

ISBN: 978-1-913499-17-4

A CIP Catalogue record for this book is available from the British Library.

Cover art ©Lebona Vernon

For Lebona and Paksie

Contents

Watching the Moon Landing on TV, in a taverna in Castile

We let the fire die,
the cheese and bread remain
untouched, beside the wine;
each heard his own heart beat;
no one could look away

as the *pinaza* beached,
and *Colón* stepped ashore
and knelt – the first to reach
and claim those talked-of lands,
with flags on upturned oars.

So much to understand:
the tapestries of hills,
heaped rain clouds, untrod sands,
dark here, but daylight there,
their bravery and skill...

He crossed himself in prayer –
God's truth: for all we knew,
that glistening strand he'd dared
sail to and land on might
as well have been the moon.

But knowledge woke that night
in us: a wind had changed.
We roused the fire. The sight
of *carabela* sails
could never be the same.

Re-reading *La Peste* in the time of COVID-19

I.

Fléau – I had to look it up – it's 'scourge':
gunshots and shouts heard faintly in the night,
and then the sound of nothing, from the hour
we woke, till darkness muffled even silence.

It means the silhouette of cranes, unmoved
day after day, against the sea and sky,
the broken cliffs that penned us in, the tides
that ebbed and swelled but carried only time.

And coffins, queueing to be tipped in layers
and heaped with lime, in ground so hard it hurt,
and seabirds, flying from and to where only
they could know, and never looking down.

II.

We were apart: from other towns,
from friends and lovers
gone before the gates were closed
or lost in layered graves,
and families of whom we feared to hear the news.

We were divorced from whom we'd been
and from the times ahead
we'd dared to see in times before –
when we'd known how to grieve.

III.

At first, when the sickness began to slow,
as birds returned, to watch us from the trees,
we couldn't remember how to celebrate.

When we'd begun to learn the art of joy again
and rediscovered how to walk in crowds
and ring the bells, a close friend died:

a soldier fallen,
as news of the armistice arrived.

Fin

The first bars are the seeds
from which the music grows,
but even the music's surprised
when it flowers; by what it knows.

The first snow lands; each further
flake that falls is laid
on the flake before, and turns
the world to white and shade:

a land that makes no claim
on you, nor yields to yours;
a shape without a name,
without an end or cause.

It's quiet, suddenly,
and the flower has set no seed.

Child

You notice things, it's true:
the wren that hasn't built
a nest to welcome spring,
the trees blown into trees
aslant, across the hill;
our lowered words of war.

You sense our fear, and ask
why we can only see
and hear through misted glass.

You notice things, it's true:
we may not be at war,
but through that clouded glass,
we hear the silence in
an unfamiliar key
and – as you quietly say –
the sky's a restless blue.

Getting out

Outside   the night's too dark to plumb
inside   the crew has cleared our meals
and dimmed the lights   the engines hum

I daren't make sense   of what I feel
I'm out at last   but can't elude
the notion   none of this is real

a frightened girl's   being interviewed
in fifties dress   three rows ahead
by men in fifties   hats and suits

who from their looks   would wish her dead
I focus on my notes   but find
my half-discovered thoughts   have fled

as has our heroine   wild eyed
lamplit   she ducks through mist-hung streets
and tries to shake   the men behind

with headphones on   I tilt my seat
play music from   another age
a different screen   shows where we've reached

an empty sea   beneath a plane
alone and lost   in empty sky
as piano   conjures soothing rain

drops falling soft   a lullaby
that helps me hide   from all I saw
but when I drift awake   our spy's

been found and caught   her eyes implore
our help but, scared   I turn away
to Chopin's lingered   open chords

and later   when I dare again
she's gone   bright sun's displaced the night
the mist has left   the movie's changed

and colour's   displaced black and white
a girl, a boy   though they're unsure
their story is   suffused with light

they lose their way at first   before
they find true love   and as they kiss
my headphones play   a final chord

and then   the window shutters lift
dawn glows   while on the seat back map:
no land nor sea   a plane adrift.

Because I know

the Earth is flat, I also know
our team brought home the cup this year
the USA's repealed death row –
our path of love's been simple, straight and clear;

hail didn't smash the apple flowers
no snails devoured our lettuce leaves
that picnic wasn't ruined by showers –
the falling acrobat caught her trapeze;

no flat tyre made us miss the plane
there was no cave-in at the mine
we've fixed the cause of climate change –
and surgeons caught your symptoms, just in time.

May

The dawn's already warm, from yesterday.
Beside the path, a thousand bees insist

on lifting every final pollen grain,
may blossom transforms hedges into drifts,

while mayweed, bruised by boots, perfumes the breeze,
and foxgloves start to hint at the colours they'll show.

Back home, our roses promise perfect leaves,
but a gap reveals where one no longer grows.

The patient tapestry of song falls still –
birds rise and chase a sparrowhawk away.

When they resume, their voices remain shrill,
in quarrel with a low propeller plane.

Is any month more beautiful than May –
or more disquieting? You seem to say.

Eulogy

He told the story of a life –
a kind of ladder that she'd climbed
from her beginnings till today

then suddenly he spoke of *her*:
her fear of all that was too vast,
from which she'd learned to hide away.

I felt you tightening with tears
and wished – again – I had the power
to touch your arm, and reach your pain.

The silent curtain glided closed
and hid the varnished coffin, where
no remnant of her presence lay.

Good value

For Audrey

'Good value', you declared, of fresh
forsythia, brightening your room.
I've heard you use those words before,
of loosestrife, primrose, gorse and broom,

in praise of plants that give so much,
though their demands on us are few:
a choir, in golden livery
of springtime, heralding the new.

Outside, the daffodils are tired –
forget-me-nots half bare their blue;
inside, you've never really known
how well your words apply to you.

Not walking under ladders

For Clare

If someone gives you a lily, a lupin, a peony –
or a fig tree, say –
convention tells you
to find it a planting space –
no matter that you never felt the need of it.

In fact, you are bound
to find it a place,
and plant it with every care,
because – alive –
it may grant you the power
to keep the giver from hurt;
and so

you sacrifice a rose,
read guides to growing fruit,
dig compost into dirt,
and spread the seedling's roots;

and water it when showers
threaten not to fall,
and train it to face the sun.

Tonight, the aroma of figs:
as warm as the bricks
in the wall
they ripen beside.

Poise

Cranesbill, clematis and rose
seek earth and sky
from an unglazed vase.

The storm has passed;
a poppy stem, weighed down,
describes a weightless arc.

The robin's love song glides
through rain-drenched air –
in rhythm with your heart.

A wave leans forward: surfing itself,
it neither breaks,
nor reaches shore.

The great cathedral dome
defies the pull
of the flagstone floor.

Each note of the requiem
combines and floats,
the perfect, only chord.

To lean,
to will to fall
but not to fall.

The arch

We didn't notice it at first,
but all the actions, glances, tics,
habits and humours we'd rehearsed
took solid form: bricks layered on bricks,
held by the mortar of our lives –
a bridge we criss-crossed, through the years.
But what connects one plane divides
the other, as Euclid made clear:
our bridge obstructed other paths
and vistas we were drawn towards,
and foiled all our attempts to pass.
So now we're left with Newton's Law:
if you attempt to break an arch
you're standing on, you risk it all.

Letter to tomorrow

When you read history books, they may not show
the many ways that people live today:
it's critical you know the things we know.

To tame a girl, her aunties pin her so
she's still, and then reduce her with a blade.
When you read history books, it may not show.

To keep them safe, we welcome those who hoe
a different row – to gardens far away.
It's critical you know the things we know.

The ragged pick among the scraps we throw
aside: the iron will never cleave to clay.
When you read history books, it may not show

up clearly, but when someone from below
makes claims beyond her due – we make her pay.
It's critical you know the things we know

to help root out the weeds that dare to grow
among your corn. Although it's clear today,
when you read history books, it may not show:
it's critical you know the things we know.

Assonance

"My Mum's an archaeologist.
 She knows how people lived before
by finding what they left behind.
 She says the atmosphere around us floats
with clues she catches in a kind
 of electronic net: a raw
and silent undeciphered mist
 of music, pictures, letters, dreams and ghosts."

Intrigued, I called the mum. It seems
 indeed, she reconstructs the past,
from disassembled noughts and ones,
 each bearing the unique and phantom trace
of those it was attached to once,
 and hers, the slow, painstaking task
of reconnecting ruptured memes,
 emotions, patterns – lives – from cyber waste.

She's pieced together damaged scraps
 of text, of film, and other crafts,
restoring tales and images
 of friendships, children, passion – loving touch.
But these are rare, all but eclipsed
 by stories lacking joy or heart,
devised for those whose mere syntax
 implies their tendency to self-destruct...

And so it happened: how they lived
 gnawing away at how they could;
their need for ever, ever more
 begetting matricidal embryos.
Result: casual unrest, ache, war;
 then timbers which had long withstood
decay and rot began to give,
 and then succumbed. As her research has shown,

before the flow of digits stopped,
  it spiked – releasing terabytes
of omens, questions, answers, fears...
  I teach my students history speaks in rhyme:
as, once again, we cannot hear
  a truth that challenges our rights;
again, we've spurned the chance to swap
  our now for maybe, nor react in time.

Patient F

From Carl Jung's notes, June 1921

I saw him, at his father's request,
on the cusp between young man and heir.
At first, he owned of no distress:
he spoke of surf and sunlit shores
but I could see the shadow there.

He walked me through a lamplit tour
of childhood, learning, family, home...
But when we reached the cellar door
he flinched and tensed with panicked eyes
at the tortured voice he heard below.

He learned to pick the lock, and find
and love the man behind the door,
and love his shadow as his guide –
in time to join the Kaiser's war
in which, enthralled once more, he died.

The lady from New England

The train pulls in. I take a seat among
the philistines and hold myself apart.
With phones in hand like zombies they regard
their messages – their work is never done –
unfortunate reminders of my son.
He trades in futures. His idea of art
is just display. To look at him it's hard
to credit where my sense of beauty's gone.

Is this what I came all this way for all
those years ago, to live among a tribe
not minding what it has? No matter: while
at work I help prepare the sales. Enthralled,
white-gloved, my fingers brush the frames, imbibe
those distant breezes, surf and sand. I smile.

The art of lost wax casting

From willing clay, she shaped their hands with hers
to reach and touch, exploring skin on skin
until they found the pose that she preferred:
a breath behind the beat, and limb to limb.

Days later, when the wax had cooled, she teased
apart the mould; the cast was true to form –
she felt the figures on her palm at ease,
and smoothed away a minor, surface flaw.

She wouldn't sell, but took the lovers home
where, ageless, they remain, held and entwined:
a single moment in the light and flow
and cadence of a lyric poem line –

a day of stolen loving, cast in bronze –
the molten touch of wax forever gone.

The house up the road

We couldn't say when it began –
a damaged window, unrepaired,
the front door varnish blistered, peeled,
a roof tile, broken where it fell?

Their daughter Jane had led her class,
excelled in music, sport and art.
They'd grown new tulips every spring,
repainted windows, swept the path.

But then their door-bell ceased to ring,
the lawn was overrun with weeds.
From dusk, a single room was lit;
all day, the curtains closely drawn.

No cause – nor outcome caused – was known:
no taxi, ambulance, or hearse
arrived; nobody entered nor
departed in the smallest hours.

Then cracks that lifted brick from brick
and seemed to know which way to turn
spread outwards in a ghost-drawn web –
a jagged, growing geometry.

I'd moved away, and later heard
the house had simply fallen in.
And when they searched the rubble pile
they found no residue of home.

See Britain by Train[1]

Two boys take turns to kick a flaccid ball
at a rotting door, deprived of the paint it needs,
as Chopin's *Raindrop* floats above the wall,
and someone's grannie wheels her shopping past
a padlocked cycle frame, entwined with weeds.

Drive through our towns in air-conditioned cars –
admire the civic flower displays, out-door
cafés and hanging baskets, fancy bars,
shops selling happy shoppers, happy fare,
clean-swept suburban streets and trimmed front lawns –

or take the train, and see the less prepared,
find time to look around, and walk those ways –
those secret passages and snickets – where
we spend our days, and buddleia, bellbind
and vetch have blown in, put down roots and stayed:

our twittens, alleys, ginnels, jitties, wynds,
cuts, twitchels, gullies, vennels, chares, back lanes –
those lurking spaces, narrow, dark, behind,
damp as the moss that grows between their stones,
or sunlit, open handed, well behaved.

We've built our towns round paths, not paths through towns,
and where you find beer cans and vetch today
was once moonflower- and leaf mould-covered ground.
Our twittens take you where they will, and show
you open secrets hidden from the roads
within their twists and turns, cut-throughs – and names.

---

[1] 1980s advertising slogan

Antiphon

You ask why that man sleeps so late
in a winter doorway, cold, alone,
as we step round him, wide awake.
I do not know.

You ask why girls your age are chased
by men with knives and guns, from home,
while you stay warmly loved, and safe.
I do not know.

You ask, why we live high and well
while others fade and sink so low,
and not give half we have to them.
I do not know.

You've asked if it's we lack the will
to act – or perhaps it's not our role?
For fifty years, I've asked, and still
I do not know.

But should you ask: by not doing more,
do we not hurt ourselves, and show
we've made a world that's deeply flawed?
Now that, I know.

Mise en scène

The afternoon had long decayed,
Scotch mist had turned to rain
and the bus delayed,

as one by one the lights came on,
and you gazed upwards,
drawn by the display
abandoned in the vacant store
across the street.

Open to view from ceiling to floor,
and brightly lit
behind rain-smudged plate glass,
the perfect family sitting room:

a buttoned leather three-piece suite, around
a low-slung coffee table where
the remote control and a scatter of magazines
had been strewn with casual care,
a standard lamp and, mounted on the wall –
the focal point – a vast
and shiny black flat screen TV.

"We could live up there", you said.
"We'd be on show, like a human zoo,
or reality TV. Or art.

We'd be muffled by glass,
but no more detached from the world
than now.
And at least we'd be looked at,
and warm."

The bus arrived.
We climbed to the upper deck,
and sat there, damp and alone,
level with the home
where you'd imagined us.

The TV was dark – its cable hanging limp and loose
on the unswept wooden boards.
A single cup had been placed
by the un-thumbed magazines,
but like chairs and settee it was empty – unused.

There's glass between us and the world, it's true,
but don't you see,
that it's equally heavy and blurred
between me and you?

A quiet town

It was Susan, raking the ash next day
to be sure the fire was spent,
who found the remains:

what seemed at first a half-burnt log
in the shape of a half-burnt shoe,
then slowly emerged as the shape of a leg.

He must have tunnelled into the heart
of the tumbled pyre of branches, pallets,
broken apple crates and tyres

when early dark had already arrived –
the shroud he needed, to hide –
and no-one there.

His mother kept on asking, of
the faces lit by fire and fireworks:
have you seen my son?

They say he'd gagged his mouth with a rag
so he wouldn't be able to scream
when the flames began.

Some people asked –
and some still do:
but why?

Newcomers mostly,
who know of the story
but didn't know him.

But we who did are quiet, today
as we were quiet, then:
remembering what we knew

and what we didn't say.
The things we hadn't said.

The sum of the day

It's cold – we claim each other's warmth
until we can ignore the claims
of light and work and land no more,
then rise, wrap well and start the day.

We follow furrows, planting trees.
Sun clears the ridge and thaws the air:
each time we pause to rest and breathe
we discard clothing, layer by layer.

Warm turns to chill as sunlight fades
and we retrace our steps to find
our jackets, hats and scarves again,
dispersed along the planting lines.

Wrapped well, we watch the night and nurse
the fire, to gain what warmth we can.
And ask: how should we judge the worth
of days that end as they began?

Waking

the night is anaesthetic
white

you draw the curtain silently
and stare

at frosted,
broken clods

and the splintered
stumps of trees

and ask no question of
the moon

The window cleaner's tale

I'd be there several times a week –
in winter, up before the birds,
as gusts of driving rain or sleet
blew slanted workers to their trains,
converging them in harried herds,

as you gazed out from your display,
blank-faced, bright-lit; and while they passed
unthinking, I began to play
a game with an imagined you,
telling you stories, through the glass:

of how Michelle and I'd renewed
our vows; of how that hadn't worked;
my new start, in a rented room...
But in reply you simply stared
unmoved, as though you hadn't heard –

until, one April dawn, you dared
the faintest smile, whispered my name
and yours; and then began to share
your stories too – of being exposed
and yet unseen; feeling ashamed

and yet ignored; decked out in clothes
you'd never choose to wear, and forced
to hold an awkward, painful pose
by those who thought you had no heart
to win or lose; and wanting more.

For months, we traded tales of scars
and wounds, weaving our dreams as one,
and stretched the hours, as rain-splashed cars
and tired commuters passed us by.
Then suddenly the lights were gone.

Instead: dismembered mannequins
lie scattered, still – seen through the lines
and hints of my reflection, in
this glass that's rigid, smudged and dark.

Peter's story

I'll tell you what compassion is, my friend –
it's when you know the crucible of pain
awaiting you, as you draw near the end,
and still elect to light the path they tread,
who walk in comfort, lit by lesser flame.

I noticed him, installed and calm ahead
of us, as we in urgent order swarmed
the carriage, took our places and prepared
to rattle through a January night
towards our weekend shelter from the storm.

Nobody spoke. In cheerless squares of light
we glimpsed the flickerings and silhouettes
of lives subordinate to evening rites
in rooms and kitchens – children, dogs and back-
yards telling tales of nurture or neglect.

We hurtled past, each held by our own track:
inflation, miners, oil, the three-day week,
the fight to keep our balance in the black.
But when the guard appeared, the traveller stirred
to speak, and puncture our anxiety:

My ticket is for greater journeys, sir –
I come from where this train begins and goes,
to sit beside you all and share the words
you know, but need to hear and learn again,
and call you to rewrite the lines you chose.

Our gaze was drawn to him, upright, restrained,
stock still in a worn, ill-fitting suit. Dawn broke
forever in his eyes – a sky ingrained
with promises – sunrise embellishing
the details of the day to come, with hope.

This crisis is the moment not to win
back what you can, but time to shake your fear
of losing all, to reach across and bring
down all the boundaries that defend your world,
and find your plenty in the space we share.

That's how he always spoke, in words that curled
around the truth until you felt it swell
and germinate within your heart. I turned
back to *The Times*, but set against its bleak
headlines... he simply drew me in. I fell

headlong, could think of no-one else all week –
his eyes, his voice, his words! – until I found
him once again, sat close, willed him to speak
and when he stood to do so felt his grace
and love reverberating in the sound.

––––––––

On better days, I simply breathe the faith
he showed and sowed in me, the certainty
with which he saw our nature, and his death,
and how our correspondence with the grain
of others' lives dispels our poverty.

What he told us in darkness, we'd proclaim
in light, he said, and I'll do all he asked,
to raise and radiate his words, his name,
and the compassion I saw in his glance
as windows rushed the sound of darkness past.

The hollow

... let this cup pass from me...
- Matthew 26: 39

This quiet is the worst:
 a hollow for my fear.

Below, the murmuring,
 above, the sky, are masked

by cedars crowding in,
 as rainless lightning nears.

My friends have yet to grasp
 the purpose in my words –

they fail to see their dreams
 as more than simple dreams;

and doze, not even half-
 aware what all this means.

All this... Was there a time
 I might have dared deny

this cup, this spell, this path –
 the hill – and turned aside?

I'm used to being alone,
 but never knew a night

so black, nor so weighed down
 with prophecy as now.

What holds me back is not
 to be no longer here

under tomorrow's sun,
  nor all the blows and cuts

and agony: it's to
  no longer be among.

Strands

The Libyans herd them through the shallow sea.
She prays, to calm the waters and her heart.
The feeble stars are blind and helpless guides
to what's in store: the fee she's paid thus far
no guarantee. They sail for Sicily.

Shells burst in silence, gunfire cuts through clouds
of sand; he spurs his men to reach the dunes.
Some do. If he survives, he'll pledge his life
to shape a peace where they are free to choose
a future far from factory floor or plough.

The castaway awakes and spits out sand –
he'll kill the bastards who abandoned him.
Then all at once he sees he knows these cliffs
and caves. The final act can now begin.
As dawn descends the slopes, he heads inland.

It's dawn. A stillness drenches sea and air.
Her uncles search the reaches of the bay.
She wills herself to will herself to fill
her heart with hope, but knows, that after days
of violent storms, the prospect will be clear.

The waves recede and in the haze a girl,
with resolute absorption, builds from sand:
a home, a street, a school, a hospital.
With certainty she cannot understand,
the callous tide returns and drowns the world.

By day, a cooling breeze kisses the shore;
at dusk, a breath of land caresses sea.
The ribbon beach divides who we once were
from every notion of how we might be:
bereaved, a priest, alone, a prince, no more...

Conspiracy

After 'The Execution of Lady Jane Grey in the Tower of London in 1554'
- Paul Delaroche, 1833 - National Gallery, London

They led you, blindfold, through the maze,
and left you, empty and alone –
and whispered as they walked away;

then later, to an injured throne
you never thought was yours to claim,
as rival families, and Rome

and Cranmer played their deadly game.
And now they lead you to the dark,
your eyes wrapped in a fold again.

The giant axeman stands apart
until the drumbeat sounds, and prays
for kind precision in his task;

as unkind Delaroche betrays
and – licensed by your mask – defiles
you with a practised, coward's gaze,

caressing you with brushstrokes, while
your unlearned searching hands reveal
the Nine Days Queen is still a child.

Catching the train from the suburbs

Today, the blackbird sings for the first time:
a warp for the robin's weft; their sonic loom
afloat in a drifted mist, its weight defined
by the delicate silence it's lifted on.

Behind, the door latch gently clicks. The dew-
drops pick out daffodils in liquid light;
the green and crimson perfect curve of new
rose stems, appearing overnight.

Fresh honeysuckle leaves unfurl in rows
of twins on tendrils searching sightlessly;
my neighbour's newly white-washed cottage shows,
in silhouette, her awkward apple tree.

I step into the dawn, and into zone
on overlapping zone of birdsong, cast
from slender branches, garden shrubs, the lone
oak's healed stub, announcing winter's passed.

A boy walks through this music more than four
decades ago. He feels, but doesn't see
the distant pilgrim, paused, eyes raised in awe,
transported by the moment touching me.

Today's the magic Leaping Forward Day
which startles us with shoots and song each year:
unheralded, obscure gives sudden way
to bright, and in this moment, all is clear.

Respite

No owl tonight, no need to fear
misfortune threatened or recalled
by its unsettled cry: stand here
and listen to no sound at all.

No planes or cars, no rustling leaves,
no murmured voices carried by
the mist; clouds merge with silent trees.
Dew falls unheard, from unseen sky.

I touch the night, it flows through me –
a dark that might have been too vast
and weightless, now sits easily;
no matter that it will not last.

Searcher

At first there is only a bank of trees;
the sky behind.
Slowly, strands emerge:
tall spears crowned with gold,
smaller, thinner wands,
and clumps, beneath.

A brisk wind snatches the tops –
rabbits snared by the neck.

Grasses mass and turn this way and that
in purples, yellows, browns,
while clouds advance with purpose –
no thought of retreat.

An eagle, gliding low
above rich grounds at the forest edge,
swoops upward, veers away;
is gone.

Its eye has caught what the wind had missed:
a searcher crouched in the margin,
noticing.

When first he'd broken cover here
he'd gathered promises:
grass stalks bent delicately green;
larks painting songs above their nests;
does, fawns and yearlings grazing awkwardly;
and tiny flowers that
mirrored and deepened the sky.

So he'd stayed,
learned where to hide, and when,
and hunted, gathered;
laid up small store.

Until the leaves began to rub and tap,
where they had whispered before:
to fall and crispen the forest floor.
The sun's path swung lower,
the starlight grew clearer,
and pierced him deep to the bone.

And now, the travelling birds have flown;
flowers have grown coy, their seeds sprung and blown.
The searcher's seen a season pass in this place,
in his home.

Fabric

Nothing has changed, and all has changed.
Your fingertips caress the land
whose weave and touch still feel the same,

the plough leaves roughness in its train
as ploughs did when these farms began
and nothing has changed, though all has changed.

October paints its glowing flames
on treetops – you reach out your hand:
their weave and touch still feel the same.

A mist still hugs the Medway plain,
pierced where spires and poplars stand
and nothing has changed, and all has changed –

past lives live on in farmstead names
though silence reigns where cowherds sang.
Do weave and touch still feel the same?

A fading heartbeat feeds the veins
that thread the wealden clay and sand –
the weave and touch still feel the same
and nothing has changed. But all has changed.

The night of the wind

This moon, two nights past its fullest,
must be shining, blue like here,
on stumps and shattered remnants
of the copse I used to walk through
on my way to you.

The spirits I once dodged
and flinched at: are they shattered too,
their shelter wrenched away – are they thus freed?
Or is their story bitterer still than ours?

Did you breathe that mushroom smell,
scuff leaves with your boots as you scavenged:
one pocket for chestnuts
and cobs the squirrels lost,
the other for ceps, and wooden whorls
or shapes that anyone else would miss?

Or did you miss all that, as I am now,
away on ventures new:
not bound in life to that small wood
as you are in
this memory of you?

When the wind came,
did you scream and freeze like Hollywood?
Or was it over before it began – bang! –
breath hurled out of your lungs
to join the assault?

Even before, in the time of those nightly walks,
there were things I failed to protect you from:
people, mostly; one in particular.
                                        But
that night of the wind –
what could I have done
but reach my hand for yours?

And now the moon shines; nights are colder.
Stumps, jagged and torn – ripped. And silence.

The seed

When you said: *don't you feel the need*
for someone to stand beside at sunset;
share those special moments with?
You sowed a seed on hard, dry ground.

But the rains were good this year, and
your seed swelled and grew.

Today: the tallest waterfall, spilt
almost casually over its lip
to thunder and rainbow spray beneath;

hot hard walk through a private ravine,
not a soul in sight;
                            and now
last licks of sunlight touch
the cliffs above my tent
as a final lammergeier circles alone,
must be a mile high.

Oh yes: the seed,
it took and grew.

I don't just need someone to stand beside,
but the sower,
to wake with at sunrise.

Sudden hill

head down
damp coal smoke
litter
grey

but when
by chance
you lift your eyes
it's there

a sudden distant hill
within the gap at the top of the rise

a place you have to go to now
a sun marked hill you've always known
a hill you've climbed a thousand times
a shrine to which you'll never go

a street lamp tries and fails to glow
and then the pavement turns again
the terraced faces harden
closing in

wet kerbstones
winter
rain

Grain

The tilth is warmer day by day
as we advance into the year,
but dusk falls early, dawn's delayed:
it's springtime, sure, but different here.

My neighbours greet me with strange words,
the sky's washed with a different blue,
birds flirt and sing, but different birds:
foretelling summer, yes, but new.

I've kept these seeds through rain and gales,
on shore and sea, through floods and snow:
if I don't plant them soon, they'll spoil.

But if I sow them and they fail,
the plough and pasture lands of home
will perish in this different soil.

Lapping

Conrad's Marlow knew
this calming, restive sound
and exiled Ovid too
and Private Gareth Jones
prone, with his fading ear to the Normandy sand
and Hawa, chained between the decks
and terrified.

They all heard water lapping –
lapping against the anchor chain,
lapping in Tomis harbour
where the galleys lay,
lapping as the gunfire died,
lapping
as the crossing plundered everything;

and reached towards where distant wavelets lapped
the shaded roots of giant, fluted trees,
the moonlit beaches by the bathhouse in Pompeii,
the dunes where schoolboys dreamed of girls in Swansea Bay,
and creeks where brothers brushed the floating rice
to fall with the driest whisper
into wooden hulls.

Each shared the sound of lapping –
shared a shore –
with those whose rippled lights reflected
worlds across the sea,
and faded, washed away by waves.

Circumstance

For Tebo

We drove through an ancient landscape
and parked.
Inside, it seemed a little cheap:
thinned out *Pomp and Circumstance* on a portable CD;
toy union jacks on plastic sticks;
the pen and blotter set from WH Smith;
the registrar in 'normal business attire'.

Through the window, rain
and the open heath
where kings and lords once rode
stretched endlessly, alongside
woodland where the deer they'd hunted hid.

Waiting: Elena, quiet, composed, alone –
her partner couldn't afford the time –
so we took and sent her photograph;
and Brad from Hove (and San Antone)
with Chris, his husband, sharing the day;
Ola and Abebi, shining, dressed to the nines;
you, in your sweater and jeans, from home –
and others from everywhere,
all sharing the day.

Elgar stopped mid-chord
and the words began: a welcome,
a note about those lords and kings – and the Queen.
But mainly about being friends,
the rights and duties neighbours share,
and lending a hand.

And then, the oaths and affirmations read:
light given weight and curved by gravity –
in the beginning, the word.

More Elgar, photographs, then time to leave,
past Births, Marriages, Deaths.

We drove our rusty car
through forest and heath,

and deer,
alert in shadows
where we passed.

His other self regrets

Apart from the first and final stanzas, this poem can be read in any order, meaning there are 39,916,800 poems here. You are invited to draw a zig-zag line at random between the stanzas, to create a reading pathway. And then try again.

If only he'd –
instead of years
spent nursing half-
imagined scars –

spent lonely hours
unsure if he'd
the nerve
to carry out the task,

seen children learn
and play the role
each chose
or in which each was cast,

passed silent villages
amidst
abandoned,
harvest-ready farms,

known deepest doubt
and lived in fear
of whom he'd find
beneath this mask

slept nights beside
and bathed in lakes
where dawn emerged
on sheets of glass,

picked hops and fruit,
and ploughed wheat fields,
and stacked hay bales
in ancient barns,

met refugees
he did not give
the help for which
they dared not ask,

awaited her return
in hopes
that every time
would be the last,

felt raindrops' touch
as balm in fields,
and bane in streets
where time rushed past,

awoken in
and then traversed
a broken desert
under stars,

climbed high through heath
and trees, to find
where frozen snow
meets scree and grass,

and stayed his disbelief
to walk
with her on their
unmetalled path.

Arabic lessons

I think I remember this:
my teacher and I discussed free will
on plastic chairs in the scent of citrus leaves,
as thorn tree shadows faded into dark.

God has no plan for you – I think he said –
but what He has, is a map of all your lives.
Which path you take is yours to choose. And then,
which path to take again. And again:

an endless web that only He could weave,
where every join and thread, once left behind, dissolves –
a web he sketched with a twig in the dirt at our feet,
explained with no more words than a child would know.

And yet, Mahmoud, you picked a course you *knew*
He'd marked in bold for you, and chose to be
a follower of given word for given word,
while most of what I learned from you's dissolved.

These towering canyon walls whose sandstone layers
were majesty, creation –
evidence that we, however small, *belong* –
have now become just weight that looms above, and walls.

The river is merely a trickle, and cold:
the sunshine barely reaches here an hour a day.
Hard to recall – imagine even – now,
the paths I chose; or those from which I turned away.

Free will embracing fate, and fate, free will:
it was all so clear, till I forgot the words.
All I can do today is greet a memory of you:
salaam aleikum, keif al hal. Shukran.

Order

He learned –
when he lived in a caravan
long ago –

the need to
fit life to the space
at home

bring back no more
than cupboards
will bear

and keep the floor
and worktops
clear.

So now when he lives
in a brick-built house
with room to spare

how is it he
can't find a place
to hide his memories there?

The return

He waves the proffered map away
and steps into the blinding afternoon:
a Sunday long ago.

The road, far wider than before,
threads new-built citadels of steel and glass
towards a spreading tree he knows.

He reaches the tree and its weaver birds,
but it's smaller
and stands where it shouldn't stand.

The path that ran downhill,
past red-roofed homes and iron gates,
climbs upward, threading scrub and grass.

A hundred yards is now a mile,
a mile a hundred yards,
with a growing thirst, he walks

from point to altered point
on ridges that had once been slopes,
and curves that ought to run straight

until – at last – at the school
and the church,
he turns that final corner, finding

tarmac where there'd once been dirt,
the distant hill more distant still,
and the fourth, familiar gate;

but a different, unfamiliar house,
neither vacant nor occupied –
no toys on the lawn.

He wants to cry
to the trees and the cloudless sky,
was it here?

But he knows,
and quietly asks
of the baked, red earth:

'If the house we knew's
no longer here,
was no-one hurt?'

Talking about God

Please stop: it makes me afraid;
afraid to think –
afraid to think there are no limits, or

there's nothing there
to place a limit on.

Even the shapes and shades
and patterns
in the flowers you brought –
they never seem to reach an end.

When I lay awake
in the Kowloon afternoon
a presence I could not consider
blew in with the warmth from the sea
and would not leave.

Back home, I'd climb alone
towards the shadow at the top of the stairs –
then turn my eyes away
and creep back down in reverse.

My friends would sign their school books:

Clapham,
 Lambeth,
  London,
   England,
    Great Britain,
     United Kingdom,
      British Isles,
       Europe,
        The World,
         The Solar System –

Stop!

While others wrote
The Milky Way, and
Space, The Universe,
I looked away.

I couldn't form the words.

Measures

'To measure is a mark of consciousness'
Heard in passing, on BBC Radio 4

1.   Ward

He's counting down from five
he doesn't know why
and fights to return
to where

it had all been green –
where he hadn't known
who was there: neither himself
nor her.

Then he remembers looking up
at a kind, efficient face:
count backwards, starting from ten,
she'd said.

2.   Ministry

Our morgues and doctors tally
all last breaths
they hear of,
hear,
or feel
on the hairs of their hands,

compile and send them here
in emails and returns
that peel away the grief,
the sudden or unfolding moments of eclipse,
relief.

We build from them a histogram –
the skyline of a nameless city
lacking history or hope –
and hand it on,

to be lit from behind by those who,
with their fading torches,
would project a silhouette
of blame, despair, success
and – yes – restore what they prefer:
grief
or relief.

3. Pasture

A shepherd doesn't count the flock,
though knows them each by name
and knows when one goes missing, or
is under par, or lame;

and when to move their grazing on,
by how the lambs behave,
and how the grass reflects the light
as dawn ordains the day.

4. Kitchen

He lays the rule and counts the marks
then checks the width and length again,
and scores and snaps the window glass –
a perfect edge to fit the frame.

But how to gauge the scope of *this* –
or know its worth – or know for sure
if it will bring us all we wish
or if it's even *this* at all?

He glances at her as she turns –
the kitchen darkened by the sun;
knows, as he overhears those words,
what they had counted on has gone.

A life of travelling

Places that stand out?
The clever answer is: the here and now, or
read my poems, you'll find them there.

But since you ask,
it's not those places where
we swam ashore,

made vows,
enriched our lives with children's smiles
and open eyes, nor

where we sheltered, awed
by falling snow; nor other moments
lovingly recalled –

but where I walked alone,
felt droplets settle, cold
upon my skin,

saw glimpses of beyond
through drifted mist
I could not disperse.

The gate

A shell obliterates
the poet's car
as young men plummet
without parachutes.

A thousand hunted girls
are put to death;
deliberate weeds
reclaim the sun-cracked farm.

When you lean backward,
what or who keeps you
from falling? What strange magic
charms your breath

to quicken you?
What is it, lets you live
and love as though yours were
a true life story?

Days are so much simpler
than we paint
them. Every dawn
a simple question gives

me pause, as I stare out
towards the thorny
wastes: to stay,
or walk out through the gate?

Things people have told me (that rhyme)

At first, I wanted them to stop
Rains flood our fields, and nourish war
They took me when I was a boy
This was a peaceful place before
And now I'm here alone

And he was gone – forever gone
We'd thought we were the chosen ones
And then I only wished to die
They came as sunset stole the sun
And night falls like a stone

They threw me senseless in the hole
When dark dissolves the moon, we pray
That woman's not the girl I raised
Now, no one knows me – nor I they
And I am here alone

Once, all you would have seen was green
It was the city made him wild
At sunrise, he could not be found
And then they killed my sister's child
And night falls like a stone

Our sons have nowhere else to go
I bled, they argued what to do
My people will not keep me safe
They say I killed my parents, too
And I am here alone

And so they joined the men with guns
And kept me there day after day
I see the life I should have lived
They left me there, and slipped away
And night falls like a stone.

Tillers

Sometimes, the poetry's a step behind:
no sooner have you coined a metaphor
of sunlit sky for peace restored, you find

it's just the calm before another storm –
a breeze becomes a wind, a gale that shakes
the leaves and bends the forest edge once more.

Sometimes, when wind-blown trees lie on the ground
a hidden bud beneath the bark awakes
and sends a branch directly to the light,

upright and eager to reform the crown,
reoccupy the sudden, empty space,
repair and feed the roots that nourish life.

But sometimes, winters can be long: unkind
and worse – unleashing storm on violent storm.

Though poetry remains a step behind,
it knows there are only so many times
a wind-torn, weary tree can be reborn.

Portent

They're everywhere this year – blown into soft,
bone dry, burnt orange heaps against brick walls
or through half-open windows onto books
and sills. They stand out clearest on tiled floors

and this white page – each one a Rorschach test,
a butterfly malformed, with passive wings
or died and pinned, a woman's labia,
a rounded cuneiform or, paper thin,

in groups they make a map of distant moons,
or atoms magnified a million times,
translucent particles divided into
two by microscopic, blood red lines.

Birch trees release uncounted seeds that glide
and flutter where – if luck allows – each swells
invisibly and dedicates a root
to burrow in the dark, drink water held

around the grains of soil, and then a shoot
and two small leaves that start the race to fill
the sunlit moments that by chance it's found.
A "pioneer", but with no art or skill –

it's just the way this tree has learned to be.
This year, its seeds are everywhere – as though
preparing for a mighty storm or fire.
What is the secret silver birches know?

Rules for rural living

a meditation at 35,000 feet

Below, a scarlet flower blooms in snow,
   predicting summer will be warm, and long;
and further south, in dunes where nomads go,
   another flower foretells hunger pains,
as Tuareg children learn, from saddle songs.

Spring's fashioned by the summer rain;
   to bruise a walnut tree, you beat its bark;
to plant two thousand seedlings in a day,
   you slice, and bend, and lift, and drop, and heel,
and slice again... and on, until it's dark;

a farmer's tread improves the barley yield;
   run sheep in camel herds, or goats with cows;
sow seven kinds of beans in every field;
   plant chillies to keep elephants at bay;
and set apart God's acre from the plough.

Clouds clear – thorn trees throw shadows on the plain;
   our engines sound a constant requiem
for when we crept up close to things, before
   we learned to see from far like Keats, who framed
his distant nightingale as metaphor,
   while Clare still saw an intimate – a friend.

Underflow

Some things, he knows – as far as knowing goes:
  the riverside address he shared with you;
those winter floods; that spring when April froze;
  the owl's call, and railway's muffled roar
that punctuate tonight, as night sounds do.

The giant nest he'd chanced on, years before,
  was perched in tree tops like a fabled shrine.
But did he also see the osprey soar
  above the pool, where dappled sunlight shone
through cluttered canopies of birch and pine?

He knows he saw the heifers and the swans
  that used to gather where the river bends
towards the bridge, through falling willow fronds –
  but did he see the cows surround the birds
and trample them, or hear it told by friends?

He knows you cut him with your sharpened words
  and dimmed the lights until he tripped and fell:
what happened in the darkness – though he's heard
  himself rehearse it many times and more –
he knows enough to know, he cannot tell...

and from the towpath, can't say if he saw
  what flowed beneath the sunlit surface, nor
the moments when swans died and ospreys flew –
  or knew the cruelty unleashed by love;
nor if the willow leaves have heard enough
  to know, the underflow is river, too.

Levelled

A fantasy of mountains
hangs above this levelled land,
a range we exhaust our last reserves
to lift and float ourselves towards
and fly among,
like figures from Chagall,
and will to become the thing again,
from which this land was made.

But as before, the soil loosens.
Softer stone erodes,
worn down by trickles, drips
and flows;
absorbing sunshine, separating
in the sight of winter stars.

And then, in the time it takes
the gods to look away
and return their gaze,
black basalt, too, begins
to starve and fray.
Granite crumbles into grains.

Mountains that rose so high
they saw horizons hold
the sea from draining dry,
fade and dissolve again – revealing
level land
and sky.

There are no gods

There are no gods –

there is no God,
                        just
this green tree,
                        in leaf
from the early rains,
                                    locusts
feeding on it.

And these clean boulders,
                                    tumbled
free of the force that held them
                                                into
an artless form they hold themselves.

But even 'green' and 'clean',
                                    and
'tree' and 'boulder':
                        such
assumptions,
                        such
blindness,

so much missed.

Prohibition

Breeze, willow, lapwing, snowdrop, combe,
brook, water, storm, clouds, clearing, moon,
nasturtium, shadow, waves, sunshine,
loch, snowfall, wren, dawn, rain, spring, tide;

learn, city, artefact, create,
fly, climb, plough, harrow, cultivate,
reveal, sustain, instil, allow,
God, wine, uncertain, free, why, how?

Distress, thirst, angry, bullet, blade,
bomb, threaten, sudden, flee, afraid,
pollution, hungry, unfair, drought,
repression, genocide, rape; doubt,

shall, schedule, may, demur, eschew,
dream, succour, susurrus, rescue,
worth, whereas, warmth, enough, enhance,
tilth, tiller, garden, silent, chance;

embrace, beside, among, with, for,
help, warn, protect, yes, reassure,
repair, touch, family, childhood, games,
home, we, I, love, you – all your names;

as news comes through, that words are banned,
we've moments to save those we can:
among the words we stand to lose –
from those at hand – it's these I choose.

The waiting room

Inside the room, I find two men:
one writes all he observes in words
that writhe and worm in argument;
the second feels and forms a world
with simple strokes of brush or pen.

I wish to know the first man's thoughts,
but all I find is darkness – so
I look towards the other sort:
all turns to white like quiet snow,
and that is why this poem's short.

Message in a bottle

When inner voices claim they've glimpsed a seam
his psyche would prefer were not exposed,
he tells them "Fuck you Freud, hands off my dreams:
a tree is just a tree, a rose, a rose."

But one can *almost* know a thing for years
(and meanwhile know it too, of course) and so
he leaves himself small clues he catches here
and there – joins up the dots – until he *knows:*

describing every day as "wet" or "dry",
a traveller passed out in a park, from "stress",
champagne for breakfast by the riverside,
sipped whisky standing for reflectiveness,

the journalist whose soul's too numb to mourn,
Judas and Jesus drinking through the night,
the drunken farmers dancing in a storm,
self-portraits with a glass just out of sight,

long games of poker in the airport bar
then incoherent flights through jagged time
and waking unsure where or who you are
to scratch away the null with wine, with wine...

Self-portrait with Jesus

There's a line in a poem I often read aloud
where Jesus, drinking wine
in a moonlit vineyard
one warm night in springtime,
touches Judas on his forearm tenderly –
beginning to say goodbye –
that when I read it, never fails
to raise a *lachrymosa* from a burial place.

But I strangle it.

Who has the right to treat themselves with tenderness?

Journey

He rides a train
through slow flat land:
nothing to see
but horizon,

wanders clumps of yellowed grass
and sand,
and sets a wounded beetle
on a stone.

With awkward clattering
a lone jackdaw
alights
and takes its unexpected prey.

Sometimes he waits all week
for a metaphor,
then two – or more –
turn up in a day.

Desert boy

`Fear the green, the rain;
Fear the shade of trees.'

Like a desert boy in the forest,
who needs time to become used to rain,
you're overwhelmed.

At first
you rush for shelter from the merest shower,
then grow brave,
and slower to flee or hide –
a glutton for water on skin,
the catching of drops on your tongue
as they run from your hair-plastered brow.

To return, now, to dust and dunes,
seems like losing
an entire camel herd to thieves.

Call to prayer

Awoken at four a.m.
by sunlight filtered through a shroud,

there is almost silence, until
beyond the open window

a robin calls the birds to prayer
and one by one they join,

as though competing to be heard, because
today is the last day;

not knowing –
or knowing, perhaps –

that no-one will be here
to recall each voice, or the song.

Acknowledgements

Grateful acknowledgement is made to the editors of publications where some of these poems have previously appeared, perhaps in slightly different form: *Allegro Poetry, Green Ink Poetry, Ink Sweat and Tears, Obsessed with Pipework, Other Poetry, Pennine Platform, Poetry Salzburg Review, The Alchemy Spoon, The Ekphrastic Review, The Kent and Sussex Folio, The Mary Evans Picture Library, The Poetry Shed, The Poet's Republic* and *Words for the Wild*, as well as the anthology *A Day in The Life* from The Hedgehog Poetry Press.

Re-reading La Peste in the time of COVID-19 was published online as part of the Plymouth and Nottingham Trent Universities' Poetry and COVID project. *Talking about God* was 'sampled' by Carl Griffin in his brilliant collaborative COVID epic, *Arrival At Elsewhere* (Against The Grain Poetry Press, 2020). *Waking* was selected to be printed as a poster on Guernsey's buses as part of the 2020 Poems On The Move competition. *Catching the train from the suburbs* was shortlisted in a Fosseway Writers competition. *Respite* was shortlisted for the Sir Philip Sidney Prize in the Penshurst Festival. I am grateful to members of the Kent and Sussex Poetry Society for their insightful comments on earlier drafts of some poems, and their companionship in poetry.

Thanks to Tebo for more than I usually say, to Lebona Vernon for his brilliant art work, and to Mark Davidson, an innovative and generous publisher.

Cover art by Lebona Vernon